BAFFLING WHODUNIT PUZZLES

Dr. Quicksolve Mini-Mysteries

Jim Sukach

Illustrated by Lucy Corvino

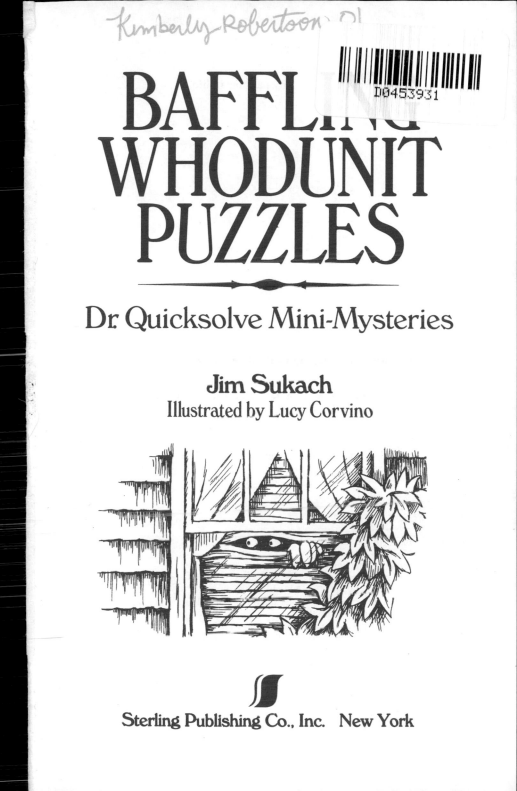

Sterling Publishing Co., Inc.   New York

For Becky—my partner in life

Library of Congress Cataloging-in-Publication Data

Sukach, Jim.
   Baffling whodunit puzzles : Dr. Quicksolve mini-mysteries / Jim
Sukach ; illustrated by Lucy Corvino
      p. cm.
   Includes index.
   ISBN 0-8086-6118-X
   1. Puzzles.   2. Detective and mystery stories.   I. Title
GV1507.D4   95-4944
                                                         CIP

10 9 8 7 6 5

First paperback edition published in 1997 by
Sterling Publishing Company, Inc.
387 Park Avenue South, New York, N.Y. 10016
© 1996 by James Richard Sukach
Distributed in Canada by Sterling Publishing
c/o Canadian Manda Group, One Atlantic Avenue, Suite 105
Toronto, Ontario, Canada M6K 3E7
Distributed in Great Britain and Europe by Cassell PLC
Wellington House, 125 Strand, London WC2R 0BB, England
Distributed in Australia by Capricorn Link (Australia) Pty Ltd.
P.O. Box 6651, Baulkham Hills, Business Centre, NSW 2153, Australia
Printed in China

Sterling ISBN 0-8069-6118-X Trade
          0-8069-6119-8 Paper

Contents

• • • • • • • • •

Dr. J.L. Quicksolve

• • • • • • • •

Meet Dr. Jeffrey Lynn Quicksolve, professor of criminology. Dr. Quicksolve retired from the police force as a detective at a very young age. Now he works with various police agencies and private detectives as a consultant when he is not teaching at the university.

He certainly knows his business, solving crimes. People are amazed at how he solves so many crimes so quickly. He says, "The more you know about people and the world we live in, the easier it is to solve a problem."

His son Junior enjoys learning too, and he solves a few mysteries himself.

Read, listen, and think carefully and you can solve these crimes too!

Bike Thieves

• • • • • • • • •

The bicycle thieves were very bold and very quick. Witnesses saw the black pickup pull up to the bike stands where the bicycles were parked. Two teenagers jumped out, raced to the bicycles, and immediately picked out the red mountain racing bike, the most valuable bike in the group. One of the thieves had cable cutters, and he quickly snapped the cable lock on the bike. The other one wheeled the bike to the truck at a run, threw it into the back of the truck, and then sped off. The whole incident took less than two and one half minutes.

The police narrowed down a small group of people in the area who owned a truck like the one used by the thieves. One was a teenager who had been brought in and was being questioned by Dr. J.L. Quicksolve. The teenager's name was Shawn, and he was asking, "What did they bring me in here for, anyway? I didn't do anything."

"What did the officer tell you, Shawn?" Dr. Quicksolve asked.

"He said a bike was stolen at school, that's all. He didn't say why they think I did it. I wasn't anywhere near the school today. I've got a truck. What do I need with a mountain bike? Who said I did it, anyway?" Shawn was very angry at being blamed.

"You have a black truck, Shawn?" Dr. Quicksolve asked.

"Yes, but so do a lot of other people," Shawn objected.

"Who helped you take the bikes?" Dr. Quicksolve asked. Shawn was stunned by the abruptness of the question.

What convinced Dr. Quicksolve Shawn was guilty?

Kenny Kidnapped

• • • • • • • • •

Mannie Bucks called Dr. J.L. Quicksolve, who came to see him right away. Mannie explained what had happened.

"Three days ago I got a call. It was my nephew, Kenny Doodit. He sounded scared, and he said he had been kidnapped. He told me the kidnappers were demanding I leave $50,000 hidden in a certain spot in the park or he would be killed. I got the money as quickly as I could, and I drove out to the park, about 10 miles south of town. I didn't see anybody in the park, so I left the money and came right home, hoping to hear from Kenny that he was safe. I pulled into my driveway and started to go into my house when Kenny pulled up behind me. He ran up to me and gave me a hug and thanked me for paying the ransom. He said the kidnapper brought the money back and let him go. Then we went in and called the police.

"They came right over, and Kenny told them what had happened. Kenny even took them to the motel north of town where they held him until they got back with the money. The police haven't caught anybody, and the whole thing is beginning to smell kind of fishy to me. That's why I called you. Can you help?"

"Yes, I think I can, if Kenny hasn't left town with your money by now," Dr. Quicksolve said.

Why does Dr. Quicksolve suspect Kenny?

Hand-to-Hand Robbery

•••••••••

The bank teller could not give much of a description of the holdup man. He was tall. He wore a dark blue coat and a ski mask over his face. He had held a silver revolver in his right hand.

Another witness outside the bank had given a similar description, but he said the suspect had held his gun in his left hand. He had also gotten a license number. The police traced the car to Bobby Bandido. They found him at home and brought him in for questioning. Dr. J.L. Quicksolve was waiting for him.

"I didn't rob any bank," Bobby protested. "I was home watching TV."

"We have a witness who saw your car and got your license number, Bobby," Dr. Quicksolve said.

"I just reported my car stolen, so you can't say I was driving it," Bobby said. "You can't prove anything."

"Maybe; maybe not. I guess we'll have to find your car."

"Besides that," Bobby went on, "you know I'm left-handed. Ask the bank teller which hand the robber held his gun in. Like I said, I didn't do it, and you can't prove a thing."

"Well, Bobby, you just answered a question I had. You're pretty smart, but I think we can prove you did this one," Dr. Quicksolve declared.

What boosted Dr. Quicksolve's confidence that he had the right man?

Gas and Guns

•••••••••

The gas station was near the freeway, but otherwise it was pretty isolated with no nearby stores or houses. In fact, it had just been robbed for the third time. Larry Loose was the clerk on duty each time. This time Dr. J.L. Quicksolve was called to investigate.

When Dr. Quicksolve got there, he asked Larry to explain exactly what had happened.

"I was just in here at the counter," Larry said, "when this guy pulled up in a blue sedan. He pumped his gas and came in as if to pay. But when he came in, he pulled a gun. I wasn't too scared because I've been through this before. He told me to give him the money, and he took it and ran out the door. I grabbed the boss's revolver and tried to catch him. I got outside just as he was pulling away. I tried to take a shot at him, but I forgot to take the safety off. He's awfully lucky he got away this time. I really had him in my sights!" Larry explained.

"Do you really know how to handle a gun, Larry?" the detective asked.

"Sure, I shoot a lot. I wasn't really gonna shoot him. I was gonna shoot out his tires," Larry said.

"I think what you really know a lot about is where the stolen money is hidden, from this robbery, and probably the other two as well," Dr. Quicksolve said.

Why does he suspect Larry?

Missing TV

• • • • • • • • •

Dr. J.L. Quicksolve arrived at the appliance store early in the morning. The manager was already waiting for him in front of the store.

"I've had several televisions come up missing recently. I think they've been stolen," the manager explained.

"Do you have any clues at all?" Dr. Quicksolve asked.

"Yes, I do. I've narrowed down the time period to the late shift when I have just two salesmen on duty. It's been the same two salesmen, Tom and Lenny, every time a TV has disappeared. I think one of them is taking the sets, but I can't figure out which one for sure. It looks like it's Tom, though I would have guessed Lenny at first," the manager said.

"Why do you think it was Tom?"

"Well, I talked to both of them. You see, with only two salesmen in a store this large, one can be in one part of the store and the other in another part of the store. They may not see each other for an hour or two at a time. Anyway, Tom said he hasn't seen anything suspicious, but Lenny said he saw Tom loading something into his trunk the other night."

"Let's ask Tom about that," Dr. Quicksolve said.

"That's him coming right now," the manager said as a small red pickup pulled into the parking lot.

"On second thought, we'd better ask Lenny what he's doing with the TV sets," the detective said.

Why does Dr. Quicksolve suddenly suspect Lenny?

Store Stickup

●●●●●●●●●

Dr. J.L. Quicksolve pulled into the parking lot of a small convenience store. Ever alert, he noticed a man in the store holding a gun on the clerk and another standing with his arms raised. Dr. Quicksolve swung his car into a parking space to the side of the lot, out of view of the three men inside the store. He used his carphone to call the police to report the robbery now in progress.

He was afraid someone might be hurt if he waited for the squad car that was being dispatched. So, with his pistol close to his side and just out of sight, Dr. Quicksolve walked into the store.

As soon as he walked in, everything appeared normal. The clerk was behind the counter. One man was standing at the counter in front of the clerk, apparently buying something. The third man was just behind him. He was standing right at the end of a row, looking at items on the shelf but not turning his back on any of the other men.

Suddenly the police siren was heard from about two blocks away. The three men all looked up toward the door and at Dr. Quicksolve. He had his gun up and aimed at the man by the shelves.

How did he know which man was the robber?

Backpacker

• • • • • • • •

"The general store was robbed early this morning. Just as the manager was driving up to the store, he saw a car pulling away. When he discovered he'd been robbed, he called us with a description of the car, including the license number. We found the car, broken down, about a mile away. It turned out to be stolen. There's nothing around there for miles but woods," the sheriff was telling Dr. J.L. Quicksolve. "So we knew one of two men we found out there almost had to be the robber. We brought them both in, but we didn't get much from questioning them."

"Did they tell you why they were out there in the woods?" Dr. Quicksolve asked.

"Yes, they both said they were out backpacking for several days. We found one campsite, and they each say it's his. There was nothing there but a small tent, food, and a burned-out campfire. We haven't been able to prove who's lying."

"What about fingerprints on the equipment?" suggested Dr. Quicksolve.

"Both prints are on different things. They both said they are away from the camp a lot, and the other one probably came in and messed with the stuff," was the sheriff's response. "And I don't think they're in it together because we can't prove they even know each other."

"We did searches," the sheriff added, "but that didn't get us anywhere either. Smith had a wallet, a folding knife, a little change, a comb, matches, and chewing gum in his pockets. Jones had a wallet, a roll of mints, a comb, a folding knife, and aspirin."

Dr. Quicksolve said, "I'd say Mr. Jones looks most suspicious right now. Why don't you see if anyone knew he was backpacking out here?"

Why does Quicksolve suspect Jones more that Smith?

Toy-Money Thief

• • • • • • • • •

"The guard called me early this morning. He said there had been a robbery here at my toy factory," Edward Elf told Dr. J.L. Quicksolve, who had just arrived.

"Let's talk with the guard," Dr. Quicksolve said.

"I was over on the east side of the building checking doors. I heard a noise, like something crashing, over on the west side of the building by the offices. I ran over there, and I saw the office had been broken into and the safe was open and empty. I could see someone getting into a car out there, but the sun was in my eyes and I couldn't see him well enough to give a very good description," the guard said.

"How much money was taken from the safe?" Dr. Quicksolve asked the guard.

"I don't know how much was there. I knew there was a lot," the guard answered.

"It looks like he got away," Mr. Elf said. "But it seems like it had to be someone who knew exactly where to go and what to do to get away with it while a guard was right here in the building."

"Unless, of course, the guard was in on it," Dr. Quicksolve said.

Why does Dr. Quicksolve suspect the guard?

Key Suspect

• • • • • • • • •

"It sure looks like somebody must have had a key to my wall safe," Al Lockitite told Dr. J.L. Quicksolve. "But I don't know how they could get it. I keep it right here on my key ring," he said. He had discovered the robbery when he came in early that morning. He called Dr. Quicksolve, who came right over.

"Do you ever lend those keys to anyone?" Dr. Quicksolve asked.

"Well, yes, I do. Two people have used the truck to deliver packages for me, John and Ted. They both work for me. They use the truck occasionally, but they always come right back after a delivery. Besides, I keep my office locked. They have never even been in there; I always come out here into the store. I like a certain amount of personal privacy," Mr. Lockitite explained.

When John and Ted came to work, Dr. Quicksolve talked to them separately. He said the same thing to each of them. "Mr. Lockitite's safe was broken into some time yesterday or last night. Do you know anything about it?"

Ted said, "He keeps his office locked up. He gives me the key ring sometimes, but I didn't get in there and break into any safe!"

John said, "What do you think? Do you think I copied his keys and sneaked in here last night?

Look at that bunch of keys! I wouldn't even know which key to copy to get into his safe!"

"Well," Dr. Quicksolve said, "we have a good suspect now."

Who? Why?

Count the Clues

· · · · · · · ·

As Dr. J.L. Quicksolve walked toward the bank, he watched a car pull over to the curb in front of it. The driver got out of the car. Without locking the door, he looked around left and right as he approached the bank. He wore a brown jacket over a blue shirt that was not tucked in and that stuck out past the bottom of the jacket. He held his right hand in the pocket of his baggy slacks, and his left hand held a small piece of paper. He wore a green baseball cap, and he lowered his head as he walked through the door of the bank.

Dr. Quicksolve entered the bank and watched the man who had come in before him as he waited for a teller. He saw the teller's startled expression, and when she handed the man a large bag, Dr. Quicksolve signaled the guard, whom he knew, and he took out his pistol.

When the man turned away from the teller, he was facing two guns. The guard's gun was pointed at his face, and Dr. Quicksolve's was aimed at his heart. He dropped the bag of money, and he slowly took the gun out of his pocket with two fingers and laid it on the floor.

What clues gave him away to Dr. Quicksolve?

Fire Liar

• • • • • • • • •

Captain Reelumin switched on the red flashing light attached to his dashboard and sounded his siren as he made a quick turnaround and sped away. He and Dr. J.L. Quicksolve had been on their way to question a suspect when they got a message about a house on fire.

They arrived right behind two fire trucks and a squad car. Another police car came up behind them. The driver turned off his siren, and two policemen got out. The back half of the house was in flames that reached up over the roof. Firemen came out the front door dragging a body. When he realized the man had been shot through the chest, Captain Reelumin began his investigation.

After the fire was put out an arson investigator

arrived. He explained how a firebomb had been used to start the fire near the back porch. Captain Reelumin had his men question the next-door neighbors while he and Dr. Quicksolve went to the house directly across the street.

They rang the doorbell and waited several minutes before a man finally peeked out the window. He opened the door and stood there in his pajamas.

Captain Reelumin showed his badge and said, "Sorry to bother you, but we would like to ask you a few questions about the fire."

Looking across the street at all the trucks, the man said, "Wow! I don't know anything about a fire. You just woke me up. I work nights and sleep in, but, sure, I'd be glad to answer any questions."

"Why did you murder your neighbor?" Dr. Quicksolve asked him.

Why did Dr. Quicksolve suspect the man?

Justin Case

•••••••••

The convenience store was robbed late the previous night. The one clerk on duty, Justin Case, was telling Dr. J.L. Quicksolve what had happened.

"I was standing here at the counter when this big guy walks in. He reaches right over the counter and grabs me by the neck with both hands. He pulls me toward him and right over the counter. Then he throws me down on the floor. My glasses fly off, and I land on my head. While I'm lying there, he goes behind the counter and takes all the money out of the cash register. He walks back around the counter. He sees my glasses lying there on the floor, and he deliberately steps on them and grinds the pieces into the floor. Then he laughs and walks out with the money."

"Can you tell me what this man looked like?" Dr. Quicksolve asked.

"No, I really can't, except that he was big. See, he broke my glasses, like I said. I can't see much of anything without my glasses. Anybody can tell you that," Justin explained to the detective.

"I think you made this story up, Justin Case. You're caught. Now tell me what you did with the money," Dr. Quicksolve said.

Why does Dr.Quicksolve suspect Justin Case?

Diamonds and Gold

• • • • • • • •

"We've narrowed the suspects down to two people, Dr. Quicksolve," explained the police officer. "The door looks like it was jimmied open, but when you examine it closely, you can see the damage really wasn't enough to get it open. A key had to be used. The only people who had a key were the two clerks working that night, Mark and Leonard."

"What was taken?" Dr. J.L. Quicksolve asked.

"Mostly diamond rings. It's funny that they seemed to have ransacked the place, but they missed a bottom drawer that held a shipment of gold rings that just came in. The gold alone is worth more than the diamonds that were taken, and the rings can't be identified easily."

Dr. Quicksolve asked to speak to Mark and Leonard separately. He spoke to Mark first.

"I left last night before Leonard did. He closed up. Everything was fine when I left," Mark said.

Talking to Leonard, Dr. Quicksolve asked, "So, Leonard, you were the last to leave last night?"

"Yes, I closed up. Mark left. Then I had to put that shipment of rings away, and I left. I'm sure I locked the door and everything. I swear I didn't take anything," Leonard pleaded.

Turning to the officer, Dr. Quicksolve said, "You'd better take Mark in. I think he has a confession to make."

Why does Quicksolve suspect Mark?

Robbem Blind,
Attorneys at Law
• • • • • • • • •

Dr. J.L. Quicksolve drove out of the gentle rain-shower as he pulled up to the gate of the parking structure. The parking attendant was just taking the money from Dr. Quicksolve when they both heard a shot that sounded like it came from the upper level of the structure. When they got to the upper level, they found the body of someone who had been shot. No one else was in the area. "Do you know who it is?" Dr. Quicksolve asked the attendant.

"Yes, it's Greg Robbem. He's a lawyer with Robbem Blind, Attorneys at Law. Their office is in this building," the attendant said.

"Call the police. I'm going to see if anyone is in their office now," Dr. Quicksolve said.

When he got to the law office, he knocked and entered without waiting. One man was there, behind his desk, cleaning up a large puddle of water that had apparently come from the open window.

"Hello," said the detective. "Are you Blind?"

"Why, yes, I am. What is it?" the man answered, blinking nervously.

"I'm Dr. Jeffrey Quicksolve, and I have bad news. Your partner, Mr. Robbem, has just been murdered."

"Oh no! What happened?" Mr. Blind cried.

"Somebody just shot him in the parking structure," said the detective.

"I see," Mr. Blind said.

"Have you been here long, Mr. Blind?" Dr. Quicksolve asked.

"Yes, I've been sitting right here at my desk for at least an hour. You don't suspect me, do you?" Mr. Blind asked.

"Yes, I'm afraid I do suspect you, Mr. Blind. Your alibi doesn't hold water."

Why doesn't Dr. Quicksolve believe Mr. Blind?"

Danny D. Seeced and Dennis Diddit
• • • • • • • •

His friends called him Danny or Danny D. His real name was Daniel David Seeced. He was dead. Apparently someone hit him from behind, took his wallet, and fled in a blue convertible, according to two witnesses who saw the mugging from across the street. The police picked up a suspect driving a blue convertible near the area. His name was Dennis Diddit, Danny's friend.

Dr. J.L. Quicksolve began the questioning. "Well, Dennis, Danny D. has been murdered. Witnesses tell us the murderer drove a blue convertible like yours. You were driving in the area. It looks pretty bad for you right away here. What can you tell us about this?"

"I can't tell you anything. I was just out for a drive. I don't know anything about anybody being murdered. There are a lot of cars like mine," Dennis said.

"Do you drive around this area a lot, Dennis?" Dr. Quicksolve asked.

"I cruise around a lot of places. But I wasn't even close to Danny D's house last night. I was at least half a mile away when the police stopped me. I never got any closer that that. I didn't even see him that night. He's not worth robbing anyway. I was just cruising around in my convertible," Dennis explained.

"Well," said the detective, "if you don't know anything about this, and you weren't in the area, you couldn't have done it."

"That's right!" Dennis interjected.

"But I don't think that's the case. I think you, Dennis Diddit, did it to Danny D. Seeced," Dr. Quicksolve stated firmly.

Why does he think Dennis did it?

Lunchtime Larceny

· · · · · · · · ·

Sergeant Rebekah Shurshot came to the door of the Winston Mansion when Dr. J.L. Quicksolve rang the doorbell. They greeted each other, and Sergeant Shurshot began to explain what she knew about the robbery of a very valuable painting. "The Winstons have been gone for the weekend. The only people who have been here, as far as we know, are the maid and the chauffeur," she said.

Dr. Quicksolve asked, "When did the theft occur?"

"It must have happened between one and one-thirty. The maid and the chauffeur had their lunch together in the dining room, where the painting was hanging, until one o'clock. The maid says she discovered the painting was gone at one-thirty. She immediately called the police. I was the only car in the area, and since this place is 30 miles from town, I was sent over here. I got here by one-thirty-five. The chauffeur was in the garage waxing the limousine. I talked to him, and he said he didn't know anything about the robbery because he had just gone to take the limousine through the car wash in town. Then I went and talked to the maid," Sergeant Shurshot explained.

"And where did she say she was between one and one-thirty?" Dr. Quicksolve asked.

"She said she was upstairs cleaning. She said she didn't hear anything. She just happened to come downstairs for cleaning supplies when she discovered the painting was missing and called the police."

"I'm not sure about that maid, yet, but the chauffeur needs to tell us a lot more," Quicksolve said.

Why does he suspect the chauffeur?

Kris Crossing Convict

● ● ● ● ● ● ● ● ●

Dr. J.L. Quicksolve was taking a short bus trip with his son Junior. They were visiting Grandpa Phineas Quicksolve in the small country town of Kris Crossing. All the way there the driver had the radio on, and the big news was the prison escape two days earlier. The escapee had been described as a young man with a beard whose hometown happened to be Kris Crossing. So, of course, this was the topic of conversation.

Junior looked around at the other passengers and quietly whispered to his dad, "You know, Dad, they usually figure an escaped criminal will return home. What if he were on this bus? Who do you think it would be?"

Dr. Quicksolve looked back at the five other passengers and said, "What do you think, Son? I can eliminate two right away, though I'm not positive about the one."

"Oh, Dad! You mean us!" Junior said.

"No, I was thinking of me and the bus driver!" Dr. Quicksolve replied.

Junior laughed and said, "Well, there are two women. It couldn't be them. The man in the back is too old, but I do see two younger men. One even has a beard. I guess he's the most likely suspect. The other guy looks like he's asleep."

"I guess I'd choose the other young man, Son," Dr. Quicksolve said.

Why did Dr. Quicksolve choose the sleeping man?

Johnnie Jumpoff

• • • • • • • •

Dr. J.L. Quicksolve knocked on the door of John and Janet Jumpoff's mountain home. No one came to the door, but he heard a woman shout for him to come in. He entered and saw Janet Jumpoff sitting in the kitchen by the phone, staring out the back window toward the sea. "He jumped off that cliff at the end of the yard! He smashed his head on the rocks below. It was terrible!"

"Your husband?" asked Dr. Quicksolve.

"Yes. John. He was upset about something. He walked out there and stood for several minutes. I was here in the kitchen making coffee and watching him through the window. Suddenly he just stepped toward the sea and disappeared over the edge! I was stunned! I couldn't move at first. Then I reached for the phone and called you. I still haven't been able to move from this spot. I'm so upset," she explained.

Dr. Quicksolve walked out the back door to the end of the yard. He looked down the steep cliff to the rocks and sea below. He could see Mr. Jumpoff's body on the rocks. Apparently he had landed on his head and died instantly.

Quicksolve walked back to the house. "I think you had better tell me the real story, Mrs. Jumpoff."

Why does Dr. Quicksolve think she is not telling the truth?

One Bright Morning

• • • • • • • • •

Dr. J.L. Quicksolve had risen at dawn, and now he was just finishing his breakfast an hour later when he got the call.

"Hello! This is Chance Taker, James Goodfellow's butler. I just got here at Mr. Goodfellow's house. Someone's killed and robbed him!" the man on the phone said.

Dr. Quicksolve arrived in a matter of minutes, and Mr. Taker brought him into the living room. There lay the body of James Goodfellow with the bright, warm sunshine that filled the room streaming across his crumpled body on the floor.

"You found him just like this?" Dr. Quicksolve asked.

"Yes, just 20 minutes ago when I came in to work. I was walking through the living room and tripped over the body in the dark. It scared me so much, I turned right around and went back to the phone there by the front door and called you," Chance said.

Dr. Quicksolve looked around the luxurious room at the leather furniture, the beautiful flowered curtains tied tightly back from the large picture window, and at the plush carpet. Finally, he said, "Throw a little light on this mystery and tell me why you did this."

Why did Dr. Quicksolve suspect Chance?

Burglar Bashing

· · · · · · · · ·

Tommy and Timmy were both nine years old. They were identical twins. Their parents seldom left them home alone for more than a couple hours. They were explaining what happened this last time when a burglar broke in. They explained that Tommy was upstairs playing with his electric train, and Timmy was in the basement target-practicing with his airgun when they heard the sound of breaking glass. Tommy ran to the top of the stairs just in time to see the burglar creeping up the stairs. Just as the intruder looked up, Tommy dropped the engine of his train directly on his head. The burglar fell backwards and tumbled down the stairs, crying out in pain.

Then Timmy ran up from the basement with his airgun. When he saw the burglar getting up, he took aim and shot him right in the forehead with the airgun. The burglar grabbed his head and ran out the back door screaming.

The police found a suspect in a nearby hospital with a bright red spot on his forehead and a gash on the top of his head that required six stitches.

"Two boys chased a burglar away about two hours ago. You fit their description of the man. You'll have to come in for questioning," Dr. J.L. Quicksolve explained to the suspect.

"I didn't break into any house, and I never saw

those two brothers you're talking about. I just fell and hurt myself," the suspect protested.

"You've given us even more evidence than the wounds and the witnesses. You're in big trouble," Dr. Quicksolve said.

What other evidence?

Alone, Ranger Robs Bank

• • • • • • • • •

The bank clerk could not give a good description of the robber because he wore a mask. But a passerby saw a car speeding from the bank and called in a description of the car and part of the license number. Two hours later a man was brought in. His car and the license number fit the description, but the evidence was not conclusive. Dr. J.L. Quicksolve was called in to question the suspect, Roger Ranger.

"The time of the robbery was about three o'clock this afternoon," Dr. Quicksolve said, and asked, "Were you alone, Ranger?"

"Yes, I was home alone. I didn't rob any bank," Roger responded.

"Yet a car like yours, including part of the license number, was seen speeding away from the bank just moments after the robbery," Dr. Quicksolve said.

"There are a lot of cars like mine, and there must be a lot of numbers that are close to mine. You don't even know if that witness got the right number down. Listen! Take me back to that bank. That clerk won't recognize me, and then you'll have to let me go. Then you can start looking for the real bank robber."

"Well," said Dr. Quicksolve, "I guess you're pretty sure you won't be recognized because you wore

a mask, but you've given us a little more evidence yet."

What was Roger Ranger's slip of the tongue?

The Foolish Hero
• • • • • • • •

Dr. J.L. Quicksolve met Officer Longarm on the docks in the shipyard. The policeman told Dr. Quicksolve there had been a shooting and a man was dead.

"Do you have any witnesses?" the detective asked.

"We arrived quickly and shut off the exits. There's little chance that the killer had time to escape. We found two men nearby. They were working in separate areas. They both say they heard the shots, ran out to the dock, and found the body lying here."

Dr. Quicksolve looked at the blanket covering the body on the dock. "Let's talk with the two men separately," he said.

They spoke with Ralph Shipslick first. "I was working upstairs in warehouse C when I heard shooting. I counted the shots as I walked down the stairs to see what was going on. I waited until I counted six shots. Then I knew it was safe to come out onto the dock. I found the body lying here. There was another guy near it. I ran back in and called the police."

"We found five nine-millimeter shell casings on the dock. I suppose one more could be someplace. It could have gone into the water," Officer Longarm told Dr. Quicksolve.

The other man was Ben Dover. "I was just walk-ing to my boat when I heard shots. I ran over here right away. I saw the body lying there, and I saw somebody run into the warehouse when he saw me. I ran back to the boat and called the police."

"Well, Officer Longarm," Dr. Quicksolve said, "If these two arc the only people in the area, one is much more likely to have been the murderer."

Ralph or Ben?

Small Change

•••••••••

Dr. J.L. Quicksolve and his son Junior were out for a motorcycle ride when they decided to stop by the police station to see their friend Sergeant Rebekah Shurshot.

When they walked into her office she was talking to a short, bald-headed man who seemed to be very upset. A young man Dr. Quicksolve did not recognize was putting money into the pay phone in the corner. He wore handcuffs.

"Are you busy?" Dr. Quicksolve asked Sergeant Shurshot.

"Yes," she answered, "but maybe you and Junior can help." She introduced them to Mr. Moneysave, the bald-headed man. Then she explained that Mr. Moneysave's house had been burglarized and the man on the phone was caught in his yard. She said he had been talking to his lawyer for 20 minutes. She also explained that jewelry and a valuable coin collection had been stolen. The jewelry had been found in the yard, but not the coin collection.

"The coins were actually more valuable than the jewelry," Mr. Moneysave explained. "I specialize in Barber dimes. I had some from 1892 to 1916. They are worth thousands of dollars!"

Finally the man in handcuffs came over to where they were talking. "My lawyer's gonna get

me out of here in a few minutes," he said.

"Is your lawyer here in town?" Dr. Quicksolve asked.

"Yes, Cheater and Sewer. Their office is just two blocks away."

"Book him, call the phone company, and let's go to lunch," Dr. Quicksolve said.

"What evidence do you have?" the young man protested.

"I can answer that one," Junior said.

What had Dr. Quicksolve and Junior figured out?

Tied Up at the Moment

• • • • • • • • •

Jonathon Abbelcore was talking to Officer Kautchya when Dr. J.L. Quicksolve arrived. Jonathon was the butler for the Duckets. "Mr. and Mrs. Ducket are in Europe on holiday," he was explaining. "I've been watching the house. I went out about two hours ago to get a few groceries for myself. When I got back I had just reached the door when a man came out of the shadows with a gun. He was tall and thin. I noticed he held the gun in his left hand. I think it was a .38. He made me let him into the house, brought me into the den, and tied me up. I heard him ransacking the house for almost half an hour. He must have been loading up the Duckets' car with stuff, because I heard him go out and come in several times. Finally I heard the door lock and struggled to get untied, but I couldn't. I was able to get the gag off my mouth and yell out the window. A guy walking by heard me and ran in here and untied me. Boy, was I glad to see him! As soon as I was untied I got to the phone and called the police."

"Did you know the man who untied you?" Dr. Quicksolve asked.

"No, I've never seen him before, and he left when he saw I was all right," Jonathon answered.

"I'm afraid you've tied yourself up in lies, Mr. Abbelcore," Dr. Quicksolve said.

Why does Dr. Quicksolve think Jonathon is lying?

Hazey Housesitter

• • • • • • • • •

Dr. J.L. Quicksolve did not get called out on a case every night, by any means. But sometimes it seemed to him that he was called out every time there was a late-night thunderstorm. This was one of those nights.

Officer Longarm met him at the door and introduced him to Hazey Story, who explained what happened.

"I'm house-sitting for Bernie and Birdie Song. They are on vacation in Florida for a week. The storm had caused the electricity to go out. I was downstairs checking the fuses when I heard a noise in the house. I walked up the stairs and looked around. I saw the figure of someone walking around taking things. I froze because I was so scared. He carried the television out to his van. I tried to call the police, but I couldn't see the numbers well enough in the dark to dial. I was afraid the lights would come on any minute and he would find me here. I hid in the basement until he was gone. Soon after he left, the lights came back on. I dialed 911 right away to get the police."

"Did you get a list of what's missing?" Dr. Quicksolve asked Officer Longarm.

"A partial list," he said. "We know about the television, the CD player, some jewelry. We'll have to wait until the Songs get home to know for sure,

though," the officer said.

"I imagine you didn't get a good look at the burglar in the dark," Dr. Quicksolve said to Miss Story.

"No, I couldn't see him well in the dark. I spent most of the time trying to hide from him."

"Yes, but even I could give a hazy description of his partner, who had better sing a different tune before the Songs get home," Dr. Quicksolve said.

What did he mean?

Foo Yoo Wonce

● ● ● ● ● ● ● ● ●

Dr. J.L. Quicksolve was talking with his friend, insurance investigator Fred Fraudstop, about various cases they had solved.

"How do you solve a case so quickly?" Fred asked his detective friend.

"Often it's just a case of being observant and listening carefully," Dr. Quicksolve explained. "Other times it's your knowledge of people, science, geography. Sometimes it just takes a little common knowledge."

"I know what you mean," the insurance investigator responded. "One of my investigators came to me one time and said our company was going to have to pay $250,000 for one piece of paper that was stolen out of a safe."

"That sounds like a valuable piece of paper," Dr. Quicksolve remarked.

"Yes, it does," Fred continued. "A Mr. Foo Yoo Wonce was a collector of rare artifacts and papers. He was especially fond of American history and American writers in particular. He collected old books, letters, and papers. One of his favorites was Mark Twain. He had gotten special insurance for his collection. One day he called and said he had been robbed. The burglar had not taken any of his books, probably because he didn't realize their value Foo Yoo Wonce suggested. He did break into the safe, though. That's where he found the valuable document, Mark Twain's birth certificate. Mr. Wonce had a witness who swore he saw the birth certificate dated 1835 with Mark Twain indicated as the newborn baby boy. We never were able to find the missing birth certificate."

"Of course, you didn't really care too much about that, did you?" Dr. Quicksolve asked, smiling at his friend.

What did Dr. Quicksolve mean?

Terry Tucker, Trucker

• • • • • • • •

Dr. J.L. Quicksolve's phone rang at five-thirty in the morning. He did not mind the early wakeup; he was used to such calls.

"My office has been robbed," his friend Terry Tucker said over the phone. "Can you meet me at my warehouse?"

Dr. Quicksolve arrived at Tucker's Trucking before Terry Tucker. Officer Longarm was waiting at the door to the huge warehouse. Dr. Quicksolve could see the door had been jimmied open.

"We got a call from a guy named Callin," Officer Longarm said. "He said he was driving by when he heard the alarm here. He called from his carphone. I just got here myself."

"Did Mr. Callin see anything?" Dr. Quicksolve asked.

"No. He said everything was quiet when he looked over here," Officer Longarm said.

Terry Tucker arrived, and they all went inside. They walked past rows of large boxes piled to the ceiling. "Televisions," Tucker said. "We're shipping them around the state."

They reached the far end of the warehouse where they found Tucker's office. His door was broken open too. They walked into the office and saw papers all over. On the wall was an open empty safe.

"It looks like they broke this open too," Officer Longarm said.

"What was in there?" Dr. Quicksolve asked Tucker.

"There was about two hundred dollars cash and my records for the past year," Tucker said.

"I can only imagine what was in those records that you wanted to hide so badly," Dr. Quicksolve said.

Why does he suspect Tucker has something to hide?

Mysterious Woman—Part I

• • • • • • • • •

Lieutenant Rootumout had called Dr. J.L. Quicksolve. He told him he had a big problem. There was reason to believe a woman burglar was in town who specialized in going to parties at the homes of wealthy people, finding the safe, and robbing the hosts.

"Do you know what this mysterious lady looks like?" Dr. Quicksolve asked.

"I actually met her at a party once about a year ago. She was blond, dripping with jewels, and wearing an intoxicating rose-scented perfume. She's known for disguises, though. She changes her hair color and makeup so well that she is difficult to recognize," Lieutenant Rootumout explained. He looked at his watch and said, "There's a big party right now. I'd like you to go over there with me and see if we can spot anything suspicious."

As they drove up to the big house, they saw two squad cars, lights flashing, at the front door. They drove on past the sports cars and limousines that lined the circular drive.

When they entered the mansion, they found they were too late. The safe in the library had been robbed. Jewels, cash, and securities were missing. One of the officers led the two men to the library. He opened the door, and they entered to

see the wall safe open and empty.

They looked at each other and both said, "It was she."

How could they know it was the mysterious woman burglar they had talked about?

Mysterious Woman—Part II

• • • • • • • •

The next day the papers were full of news of the mysterious woman thief with the rose-scented perfume. Dr. J.L. Quicksolve knew he had lost a clue. She would be too smart to wear that recognizable perfume again soon.

The next Saturday they had to deal with the added problem of two big parties on the same night. Dr. Quicksolve would be at one party, and Lieutenant Rootumout would be at the other. A police officer would be placed at the door where the jewelry and money were kept at each house.

Dr. Quicksolve circulated among the guests and was careful to meet every woman there. They were all known to the host. He found no one suspicious. At about ten o'clock he got a call from Lieutenant Rootumout. That house had been robbed. Dr. Quicksolve hurried over.

Lieutenant Rootumout met Dr. Quicksolve at the door. "I had a good man standing at the door of the bedroom. I don't know how the thief got past. We found the host of the party knocked out in his room."

The butler told Dr. Quicksolve he saw the host go up to his room with an attractive blonde in a black dress. A short time later, he said, the policewoman came running down the stairs and told him to call the police. She said she would try to

catch the thief and ran out the back door.

Dr. Quicksolve, Lieutenant Rootumout, and the butler stood in the bedroom looking around. Lieutenant Rootumout walked to the open window and looked down. "Too far down to jump," he said. They heard a muffled noise from the closet.

"I know how she got away, but excuse me now. I have to get back to the other party," Dr. Quicksolve said before quickly exiting the room.

What does he suspect? What was the noise from the closet?

Mysterious Woman—Part III

• • • • • • • • •

Dr. J.L. Quicksolve hurried back to the party he had been at earlier that night. He found there were two attractive blondes who had not been there before. They both wore black dresses. The only difference was that one wore a mini-dress, and the other one a floor-length gown. Speaking to the host, Dr. Quicksolve learned the host did not know either woman and they had not spoken to anyone since they arrived just a few minutes before Quicksolve's return. He spoke to each of them.

The woman with the floor-length gown said she was late to the party because she had a flat tire on the highway and had to call road service.

Dr. Quicksolve worked his way toward the second woman, the one in the mini-dress. He greeted several people who recognized him as he crossed the room. He finally reached the beautiful woman standing alone and asked why she was late to such a wonderful party. She said she had started out and then noticed a tear in her dress. She had to turn around and go back home to change. Then she excused herself, saying she needed to go to the ladies' room. Dr. Quicksolve watched her wend her way through the crowded room and climb the stairs.

The detective turned to look at the first woman.

Then he quickly phoned Lieutenant Rootumout. "I found her," he said into the phone.

How did Quicksolve know which one was the thief?

Dup and Strong

• • • • • • • • •

Dr. J.L. Quicksolve took the elevator up to the second floor and knocked on the door of apartment number 216. Officer Longshot opened the door and let him in. He introduced Dr. Quicksolve to two men. Bill Dup was tall and broad shouldered. Les Strong was short and thin and wore thick glasses. Officer Longshot said Bill was working out at his health club and Les was in their apartment at the time of the incident. "I'll let Les tell

you the story," he said.

"Actually, I was just coming in when I was struck from behind and knocked to the floor," Les said. "There were two strange men. Before I could get up, one grabbed my arms. The other guy taped my mouth shut so I couldn't call for help. I have a cold, and I could barely breathe. They tied me to a chair, took my wallet, and got the money out of it. They opened our wall safe there behind the picture of Bill's girlfriend and took the money. Everything happened so fast, and I was woozy from the hit on the head and the trouble I had breathing. They moved fast and were out of here in about three minutes."

"I got here about 20 minutes ago and found Les tied up," Bill said as he worked the combination of the wall safe. "I passed two men on the stairs on the way up, but I didn't know them. They must have been the thieves." He turned the dial back and forth and opened the safe as he spoke. "You're right, Les. They took all the money." Turning to Dr. Quicksolve, he said, "I had three thousand dollars in there. I was buying a used car, and the guy would only take cash. I was going to pick up the car in the morning."

"I think we are hearing less than the truth here," Dr. Quicksolve said.

Why does Quicksolve suspect a lie?

Hot Toddy

• • • • • • • • •

Dr. J.L. Quicksolve drove down a dark stretch of road. He was on his way to a convenience store for hot-dog buns. He passed a police car that had stopped a dark sedan. Dr. Quicksolve waved to the policeman as he drove by.

On the way back home Dr. Quicksolve noticed the police car and the dark sedan were still parked on the side of the road. He wondered if he could help and pulled his car to the other side of the road. Crossing the street, he saw the policeman talking to a young woman and a young man who seemed to be intoxicated.

"Drunk driving?" Dr. Quicksolve asked when he walked up to the police car where the officer seemed to be reluctantly writing a ticket.

"Dr. Quicksolve!" the policeman said, recognizing the famous detective. "That's what I figured, but this young woman claims she was driving, even though she doesn't have a license. I don't believe her. I think she's trying to keep her boyfriend from getting into even more trouble for driving drunk."

"Tell me your story," Dr. Quicksolve said to the woman, who was sitting in the back of the police car next to her boyfriend.

"We were at a party. I told Toddy not to drink so much. He kept saying he was hot and needed to

drink to cool down. I told him if he was drinking, I'd better drive. He said okay and gave me his keys. I know how to drive because I watch my dad. I just put my foot on the clutch, turned the key, put it in 'D' for drive, and away we went. I swerved in the lane a little, but I stayed on my side of the line. At least we were safe," she explained.

"I think you can make that drunk driving charge stick, officer," Dr. Quicksolve said.

Why was he so sure?

Missing Motorcycles

Dr. J.L. Quicksolve held a newspaper over his head as he sloshed through the puddles in the pouring rain and entered the front door of Max's Motorcycles. The place was nearly empty except for three desks and several chairs.

"He took every motorcycle in the place," a bearded man sitting at one of the desks was telling Officer Rebekah Shurshot, spreading his arms in frustration at the emptiness of the room.

Seeing Dr. Quicksolve, Officer Shurshot stood up and introduced him to the owner, Max Hardsaddle.

"Who is *he?*" the detective asked, pointing, and getting right to work.

"Tom Shifter," Max said. "He works for me as a salesman. I found his credit card on the ground outside, right in front of the door. Apparently, he used it last night to open the door and rob me. He must have had a big truck and somebody to help him. I should have fired him a week ago."

"Was he a bad worker?" Dr. Quicksolve asked as he examined the deadbolt lock on the front door.

"He didn't sell much. Nobody did. I was in trouble already."

Tom Shifter came in, and Dr. Quicksolve questioned him privately. "I didn't steal anything," Tom said. "What would I do with all those bikes?

I lost my wallet and credit card a week ago. I thought I lost them here at work, but I couldn't find them."

Dr. Quicksolve walked over to Max and said, "Well, Max, I guess you figured you could get the insurance money for the motor cycles and then sell them cheaply to someone else, eh?"

Why does Dr. Quicksolve suspect Max is lying?

High Voltage

• • • • • • • • •

Dan Voltage's name was all over the newspapers. This local eighth-grade science teacher had just discovered an inexpensive way to turn water into gasoline. His spirits were high, and he was certain to make millions of dollars with his new process. Now his name would be in the paper for another reason. He had been kidnapped.

Dr. J.L. Quicksolve, his son Junior, and Lieutenant Rootumout were at Voltage's house talking with Mrs. Voltage. Dr. Quicksolve and Junior had been watching a soccer game in a drizzling rain when Lieutenant Rootumout paged the detective. They had come straight from the soccer game. "I was shocked when I got home and found this note," Mrs. Voltage explained.

Lieutenant Rootumout read the note: "If he gives us the formula, we will let him go. Do not try to find us."

"He was here a few hours ago when I left to go shopping," Mrs. Voltage said. "As I drove away I saw our neighbor, Brace Yaseph, and another man pull into our driveway in a van."

Dr. Quicksolve walked from room to room, looking for clues. On the kitchen table was a bottle of lemon juice and a glass filled with what looked like lemonade. If there had been ice, it had melted. There was a basket containing grapes, bananas,

and apples. Next to that lay a sheet of paper and a toothpick. In the living room he noticed an ashtray filled with cigarette stubs. "Does your husband smoke?" he asked.

"No, he never smokes," Mrs. Voltage answered.

"If someone has a match, we might find Mr. Voltage," Junior said from behind them." Lieutenant Rootumout looked puzzled. Dr. Quicksolve smiled.

What did Junior have in mind?

If Fish Could Talk

• • • • • • • • •

Dr. J.L. Quicksolve was eating donuts at the Donut Shop with Officer Longshot and a few local friends when a call came over Officer Longshot's portable radio. There had been a murder nearby. Dr. Quicksolve took his donut with him.

The manager let Dr. Quicksolve and Officer Longshot into a large, expensive apartment on the eighth floor of the huge apartment building. The

apartment was a mess. Kitchen cupboards were open. Dishes were broken and scattered. Cushions from the couch were on the floor. Chairs were turned over. Rock music came from the stereo, and the body of a man lay in the middle of the floor. A knife was in his back. Two goldfish were circling monotonously in a small, clear fishbowl, ignoring the outside world. "If they could only talk," Officer Longshot said.

The manager, Mr. Keyperson, said, "He's Donald Deadman. He's lived here for several years. I found him like this a few minutes ago. He was planning to go to Chicago tomorrow with his friend who had been here for several days. He wanted me to keep an eye on things, water his plants and stuff. I was going to ask him about it. When he didn't answer the door I thought he might have left early. I came in to see if he had gone already. It looks like he caught a burglar in the act."

"Do you know who his Chicago friend is?" Dr. Quicksolve asked him.

"Yes, I have his name and his license number. We try to keep track of overnight visitors."

"Good," Dr. Quicksolve said. "Have the Chicago police track him down," he said to Officer Longarm. "This wasn't a burglary."

How does Dr. Quicksolve know this was not a normal burglary?"

Murder Lake

• • • • • • • •

Dr. J.L. Quicksolve had no sooner cast out his lure when something hit his line that almost pulled the fishing rod from his hands. Suddenly he heard "Bam! Bam! Bam! Bam! Bam!"

"Sounded like gunshots," said his friend Fred Fraudstop.

Dr. Quicksolve felt his line go slack as his fish got away. "Yes, it did," he said, looking at the lake around him from the little cove where they were anchored deep in the lily pads. "Let's check it out."

They rounded a little projection of land that jutted out near their fishing spot. Now they could see more of the lake. A man was standing in a boat at a dock behind a huge house. The house was surrounded by flowers and colorful shade trees. Long, wide concrete stairs led from the house down to the dock. As they came closer, they saw what looked like a body slumped over the backseat of the motorboat the man was standing in.

Dr. Quicksolve identified himself, and the police arrived quickly. John Joyboat said he had been out for a ride with his uncle in his motorboat. They were just coming back into the dock when a man on the dock shot his uncle. "He had a nine- millimeter automatic," Joyboat said. "He shot once from the dock. Then he took a couple steps back to the stairs there and shot several more times before he ran away past the house."

"How do you know it was a nine-millimeter automatic?" Dr. Quicksolve asked him.

"I have one. I mean I had one like it. It was stolen about a month ago," Mr. Joyboat said.

Dr. Quicksolve walked slowly back and forth across the dock and the stairs, looking down intently. "Arrest him, officer," he said. "You had better search him and the boat. You might have to call for divers."

What was Dr. Quicksolve talking about?

Last Walk

• • • • • • • • •

It was a nice day for a walk in the park, but it is never a nice day for a murder.

Dr. J.L. Quicksolve pulled his collar up and stuffed his hands into his coat pockets as he stood in the Metropolitan City Park talking to Officer Longshot. They stared down toward a man's body lying in a shallow gully below them. The leaves swirled around their feet as the autumn air cooled their unprotected faces.

"That's C.U. Later," Officer Longshot said. "It looks like he fell and hit his head. His wife is in my car. She just identified the body. She's pretty upset. They live about five blocks from here, up into town."

"Could it have been a blow to the head that killed him?" Dr. Quicksolve asked.

"Sure, as far as I know. Mrs. Later said her husband went out to walk the dog. They had a fight. He threatened divorce. She said he was just upset about losing his job."

"Who found the body?"

"She did. She said she was out looking for him because she was worried."

They heard a bark behind them and turned to see a small beagle run by the police car. Mrs. Later stepped out of the car and called the dog, who apparently recognized her voice and came running to her. She bent down, hooked a leash to his collar, and hugged the dog. She removed a glove to reach into her jacket pocket and gave some kind of treat to the dog.

"Well, there's the dog to back up her story," Officer Longshot said.

"No, I'm afraid her story is not to be believed," Dr. Quicksolve replied.

Why does Dr. Quicksolve suspect Mrs. Later?

Early-Morning Crime

•••••••••

"Look at this!"

Shortstop, Quicksolve Junior's best friend, was upset. He was pointing to his locker, which had been so badly damaged it could not be closed. "Someone broke into my locker and stole my jacket!"

Junior surveyed the scene. The locker had been forced open with some kind of a prybar. It must have taken a while. About a dozen or more red pistachio shells lay in front of the locker. One or two shells were inside it. An empty cola bottle was on the floor.

"It looks like the culprit had a snack while he pried it open," Junior said.

"Yeah. That stuff wasn't there when I went to class," Shortstop said.

"Second hour hasn't started yet, so it obviously happened during first hour," Junior thought out loud.

They went to the principal and reported what had happened. He said several lockers had been broken into in the past week. Junior suggested he question everyone who was out of class during first hour. The principal called the teachers over the public address system, and four kids were sent to the office.

Junior peeked at the four suspects from the

principal's office. He knew all four. Prissy Powers
was the cutest girl on the cheerleading squad. She
had to brush her hair and check her makeup at
least once an hour. Dennie Dos, the computer
expert in the school, sat twiddling his thumbs.
John Bigdood had a reputation as a bully, but he
had never been caught stealing. He sat there with
his band gloves on, drumsticks in hand, playing an
imaginary drum. Art Full was doodling on a
notepad. No one looked happy about being sent to
the office.

Junior turned to the principal. "I think I know
who did it, and I can prove it," he said.

Who? How?

Hopalong

• • • • • • • • •

Junior looked around at the small Texas town in amazement as he rode slowly down the main street on the back of his father's motorcycle. A large banner stretched across the street said, "Hopalong Cassidy Days."

"This looks like a town straight out of the Old West!" he said to his dad.

Dr. J.L. Quicksolve turned his head and said, "It sure does, except for the cars and the neon lights."

Junior noticed there were even horses tied up in front of several places, including a saloon, where a crowd had gathered. The Old West picture was spoiled, though, by the flashing lights of a yellow ambulance and a white police car with a large gold star on the door. Naturally, Dr. Quicksolve pulled up, parked his motorcycle, and got off to see what

happened. He expected the man he was here to see, his old friend, Sheriff Sam Sixshot, would be on the scene.

He was right, and after warm greetings, Dr. Quicksolve introduced his son Junior to the sheriff. Then they got down to business. A man named Slim had been shot in the back in front of the saloon. Dusty Throte was the only one who saw anything.

"I was walking toward the saloon, about half a block away. I saw a guy in a black outfit come out of the saloon, turn right, draw a gun, and shoot Slim down just as he lifted his foot into the stirrup to get on his horse," Dusty explained, pointing to a white horse standing there facing the buildings. It was tied to a hitching post about 20 feet from the door of the saloon.

"That's not much of a description," Sheriff Sixshot said, "considering half the men in town are wearing black outfits today to celebrate Hopalong Cassidy Days."

Junior looked around, a little disappointed in himself for not noticing all the men in black cowboy outfits and white hats. Then he perked up and said, matter-of-factly, "But we don't really need to know anything else, do we, Dad?"

What had Junior figured out?

Lester Mesterup

• • • • • • • • •

Patti Pug had been assaulted and robbed. "I was walking home from work. It was about five o'clock," she told Dr. J.L. Quicksolve and Captain Reelumin. "Suddenly a man came up from behind me, grabbed my shoulder and hit me in the face. He took my purse as I fell. Then he ran away."

She said she got a good look at the man and would recognize him if she saw him again. Captain Reelumin had the known thugs in the area rounded up and brought in for questioning on suspicion of robbery.

When the suspects were lined up, Patti stood and pointed at Lester Mesterup. "He's the one!" she said.

Captain Reelumin and Dr. Quicksolve questioned Lester in another room. "Where were you at five o'clock yesterday afternoon?" Captain Reelumin asked.

"I went out for a walk," Lester said. I didn't rob anybody." He avoided Dr. Quicksolve's eyes.

"You've done it before, Lester. That's why we have to be suspicious when it happens right in your neighborhood," Captain Reelumin said.

"Do you go for walks a lot?" Dr. Quicksolve asked him.

"Yeah, I go for a lot of walks. I walk my dog every day. He needs the exercise. I was walking my dog," Lester explained.

"How long did you walk?" Dr. Quicksolve asked.

"About an hour. I walked about an hour," Lester said.

"It's more than a hunch when I say it should be easy to prove Lester is guilty," Dr. Quicksolve said.

Why?

Backstab

· · · · · · · · ·

Dr. J.L. Quicksolve had been called on his car-phone and arrived at Barney Blarney's house ahead of the police. It was a white Cape Cod house. The morning sun glistened from the windows.

Barney unlocked the front door and let the detective in. Dr. Quicksolve explained who he was and asked Mr. Blarney to tell him what had happened. Barney was a small, worried-looking man who looked even smaller in his over-sized pajamas. He seemed to be quite upset and had trouble speaking at first. He took Dr. Quicksolve into the kitchen at the back of the house and showed him

the body of his brother, Pat, lying on the floor. Pat's madras pajamas matched the ones his brother wore, except for the large blood stain where a kitchen knife protruded from his back.

"My brother's been stabbed," Barney finally said. Then he showed Dr. Quicksolve an open window in the utility room just off the kitchen. The latch was broken and the window frame was damaged. "He came through the window here," Barney said. "The back door is still bolted."

Dr. Quicksolve looked out the window at the ground which was wet and muddy from the night rain. He saw a set of clear, large footprints leading up to the window. There was also mud on the kitchen floor.

"Somebody broke into the house and killed him early this morning," Barney said. "By the size of those tracks, You can see it must have been a big man," Barney said.

"Did you search the house?" Dr. Quicksolve asked Barney.

"There's no one," he said as the doorbell rang. "That must be the police," he added as he walked toward the door

"Get dressed, Mr. Blarney. They will be arresting you and taking you down to the police station."

Why did Dr. Quicksolve think Mr. Blarney would be arrested?

Baubles

• • • • • • • •

An old-fashioned bell rang out when Dr. J.L. Quicksolve turned the knob and opened the door to the old jewelry store. The store owner, Berry Opal, greeted Dr. Quicksolve with a handshake. The jewler suspected his clerk after the third robbery in six months. All three robberies had taken place while this same clerk was working alone in the jewelry store. Mr. Opal asked Dr. Quicksolve to talk to him.

"After the first two robberies," the clerk explained to Dr. Quicksolve, "I decided to bring my gun to work. I'm pretty good with a pistol, and I wear it here under my jacket. I just did not get a chance to use it. The thief had a gun, or at least he said he did. He had his hand in his pocket, and I couldn't take a chance with his hand already on his gun like that. If I had any chance to get the drop on him, I would have stopped this robbery and saved my job! I'll never forget what he looked like: tall, bald-headed, with a big handlebar mustache. I'll probably be fired now, even though I didn't have anything to do with the robbery. It's just been bad luck that I've been here when the place gets robbed."

"I understand the thief got away with quite a lot this time," Dr. Quicksolve commented.

"Yeah, two large bags of jewels! He could hardly

carry it all, but he wasn't about to let go of them! We had just recently replenished our stocks from the last robbery. We were even stocked up extra for a sale," the clerk explained. "I don't know what I'll do if I lose this job!"

"At least you will have a place to stay and three square meals a day," Dr. Quicksolve said.

What did Dr. Quicksolve mean?

Answers

• • • • • • • • •

Bike Thieves (page 6)—Shawn knew it was a mountain bike that was stolen even though no one had told him.

Kenny Kidnapped (page 8)—Kenny could not have gotten to his uncle's house so quickly if the kidnappers picked up the money 10 miles south of town and drove to a motel north of town with it before they let him go. Kenny must have been in on this trick to get money from his uncle.

Hand-to-Hand Robbery (page 10)—Apparently, Bobby had this well planned. He phoned in about his car being stolen. He also switched the gun to his right hand for the robbery and back to his left when he thought no one could see him. Then he tried to use left-handedness as an alibi, admitting he knew the robber used his right hand.

Gas and Guns (page 12)—There is no safety on a modern revolver.

Missing TV (page 14)—Lenny said he saw Tom put something in his trunk, but Tom drives a pickup. Lenny must be lying.

Store Stickup (page 16)—He knew the robber would not have let any of the other men get behind him when he tried to make everything appear normal when Dr. Quicksolve came into the store.

Backpacker (page 18)—It's unlikely anyone would go camping for several days without matches to build a campfire and cook.

Toy-Money Thief (page 20)—The guard claims he could not see the robber because the sun was in his eyes, but he was on the west side of the building looking out the window. In the early morning the sun is low in the east. It could not have been shining brightly in his eyes!

Key Suspect (page 22)—Ted responded with the phrase "break into any safe," but John seemed to know a key was used. He said, "I wouldn't know which key to copy to get into that safe!" If he had not been in the office, John would not have known the safe took a key and not a combination. John is the suspect!

Count the Clues (page 24)
1) He left his car unlocked for a quick getaway.
2) As he went into the bank, he checked around for police or anything else that might hinder his getaway.
3) His right hand held the gun in his pocket so it would not bounce around, so no one would notice the outline of a gun in his pocket, and so he could draw the gun quickly.
4) He also wore baggy clothes with his shirttails out to hide the gun in his pocket.
5) A bank robber often wears a baseball cap because the long brim helps cover his face.
6) He also lowered his head to keep his face out of sight of cameras and witnesses.
7) Quicksolve watched the teller's face for any sign of shock or fear as she read the note. This was the strongest clue.
8) The final clue was the large bag of money which took on special significance because of all the other clues that he had already seen.
   Did you find any more clues?

Fire Liar (page 26)—Wow, indeed! This neighbor claims he slept through a gunshot, a firebombing, and at least five emergency vehicles with screaming sirens and flashing lights practically in his front yard! There is good reason to doubt him.

Justin Case (page 28)—Justin explained that the robber walked right up to him and grabbed him by the neck. Then he pulled Justin even closer to him. This all happened before Justin's glasses were knocked off! He should have been able to see the robber clearly and give a good description.

Diamonds and Gold (page 30)—If Leonard were the thief, he would have taken the valuable gold rings. Mark overlooked them when he came back to rob the store because he had left and did not know they had come in.

Robbem Blind, Attorneys at Law (page 32)—If he had been sitting at his desk the past hour, he would have closed the window sooner and prevented a gentle shower from making a large puddle.

Danny D. Seeced and Dennis Diddit (page 34)—Dennis said he knew nothing about the murder, yet he knew Danny was robbed.

Lunchtime Larceny (page 36)—The chauffeur claims he drove to town, 30 miles away, to wash the car. Yet, he was there waxing the car at one-thirty-five. He could not have made the 60-mile round-trip in 35 minutes, so he must be lying about where he was during the time of the robbery.

Kris Crossing Convict (page 38)—The escape was two days earlier. The convict would have shaved, to eliminate the most obvious clue to his identity.

Johnnie Jumpoff (page 40)—Mrs. Jumpoff knew about the head injury, yet she claimed she had not left the kitchen to look down the cliff.

One Bright Morning (page 42)—Chance said he tripped in the dark long after sunrise in a brightly sunlit room.

Burglar Bashing (page 44)—The man knows the boys are brothers only because he saw them during the burglary, and they look just alike.

Alone, Ranger Robs Bank (page 46)—He said to take him back. He could only go "back" if he had already been there. In this case he had already been there robbing the bank.

The Foolish Hero (page 48)—Ralph said he waited until he heard six shots. He does not know much about modern guns, especially nine-millimeter weapons. Most of them are automatics and fire at least eight shots. He was foolish to come running after six shots. The person who owned the gun and shot the man would have known better. Ben Dover is the more likely suspect.

Small Change (page 50)—The young man was on the phone making a local call for 20 minutes. Junior and Dr. Quicksolve knew he should not have needed to put more money in as they came in. They figured he was getting rid of the evidence. Dr. Quicksolve wants the phone company to open the coin box to find the missing dimes.

Tied Up at the Moment (page 52)—Jonathon said the robber locked the door, yet a stranger walking by was able to just run into the house.

Hazey Housesitter (page 54)—Dr. Quicksolve suspects that Hazey is the burglar's partner and that she is not telling the truth. Someone who could see well enough in a dark house to move around as much as she did and who knows to dial 911 could figure out where the 9 is on the dial just by counting. The one, of course, is very easy to find.

Foo You Wonce (page 56)—Dr. Quicksolve knew that if there were a birth certificate for Mark Twain, it would be a worthless fake. Mark Twain was a pen name used by a man born with the name Samuel Langhorne Clemens.

Terry Tucker, Trucker (page 58)—Tucker said his office had been robbed when he had no way of knowing that. He only knew the alarm had sounded. It also looks very suspicious that burglars would settle for two hundred dollars and some papers and pass up thousands of dollars worth of televisions. Tucker had something in his records he wanted to hide, so he staged the robbery.

Mysterious Woman—Part I (page 60)—Although the big party and the open safe were clues, the big clue was not what they saw. It was what they smelled: the intoxicating rose-scented perfume.

Mysterious Woman—Part II (page 62)—Dr. Quicksolve realized Lieutenant Rootumout said he had a "good man" at the bedroom door. The butler said a policewoman ran down the stairs. The thief must have been that woman in the policeman's uniform. Dr. Quicksolve is now afraid she headed for the other party.

Mysterious Woman—Part III (page 64)—The first woman had a legitimate excuse. She probably used her carphone to call for help. The second woman is the thief. Neither woman was known by the host or had spoken with anyone at the party. Yet the second woman knew exactly where the restroom could be found. Being a professional thief, she had learned about the house somehow before she got there. Unfortunately, she escaped somehow from a second-floor window before Dr. Quicksolve reached the restroom. She had audaciously left a black silk scarf on the windowsill. It had the strong scent of roses.

Dup and Strong (page 66)—Les could not have told the robbers the combination of the safe with his mouth taped shut. They could not have opened it and gotten away in three minutes without the combination. Les must have helped his friends get Bill's money and faked the rest.

Hot Toddy (page 68)—The girl said she pressed the clutch and shifted into "D," for drive. A car with a clutch pedal would not have a gear marked "D." "D" is for drive with an automatic transmission. There would not be a clutch pedal.

Missing Motorcycle (page 70)—The credit card method of opening a locked door does not work with a deadbolt lock.

High Voltage (page 72)—Junior knew Voltage was a science teacher, and he remembered something he had learned in science class when he looked at the table. Lemon juice makes good invisible ink, and you can use a toothpick to write with it. Sure enough, when he passed a lighted match under the sheet of paper, the words "YASEPH'S COTTAGE" appeared. Lieutenant Rootumout sent some officers to Yaseph's cottage in the mountains where they rescued Mr. Voltage.

If Fish Could Talk (page 74)—A professional burglar would not go through the dishes, and he probably would have taken the stereo. So much damage looks like someone wanted the police to believe it was burglary.

Murder Lake (page 76)—Dr. Quicksolve knew an automatic would spit out empty shells as it was fired. Since he found no shells, he figured Mr. Joyboat did the shooting from the boat. If no gun were found on him or the boat, he probably threw it in the lake.

Last Walk (page 78)—If Mr. Later had been walking the dog, it would still have a leash attached to its collar as is required by most cities and parks. Apparently, Mrs. Later was worried about her husband's lost job and a possible divorce and decided to settle for his life insurance.

Early-Morning Crime (page 80)—Junior suspects John Bigdood. He has his drumsticks as an excuse to wear his band gloves, which cover his hands so no one can see the red stains on his fingers from the pistachio shells.

Hopalong (page 82)—Dusty said Slim had just raised his leg to the stirrup to mount his horse. He also said the killer turned to his right as he came out of the saloon. If both things are true, a man exiting the saloon like that could not have shot Slim because his horse would have been between him and the saloon door. Dusty must be lying.

Lester Mesterup (page 84)—The victim identified Lester, but she did not mention a dog. If Lester was walking his dog for an hour around five o'clock in the afternoon, someone would have seen him. If anyone saw him without the dog, it would be more proof he is lying.

Backstab (page 86)—Barney was anxious to point out the tracks could not be his because they were too big, yet the tracks led into and not away from the house, and the doors were locked. He must have used large shoes to make the footprints so he would not be suspected.

Baubles (page 88)—He meant the clerk was probably headed for jail. It sounds like he was lying when he said he never had a chance to pull his gun and get the drop on the thief. Dr. Quicksolve could not picture how a bandit could carry two heavy bags and turn the knob to open the door to leave with one hand kept in his pocket.

Index